I0470731

The Key Facts™ on

Egypt

Essential Information on Egypt

By Patrick W. Nee

The Internationalist®

www.internationalist.com

The Internationalist®

International Business, Investment, and Travel

Published by:

The Internationalist Publishing Company

96 Walter Street/ Suite 200

Boston, MA 02131, USA

Tel: 617-354-7722

www.internationalist.com

PN@internationalist.com

Copyright © 2013 by PWN

Table Of Contents

Chapter 1: Introduction

The regularity and richness of the annual Nile River flood, coupled with semi-isolation provided by deserts to the east and west, allowed for the development of one of the world's great civilizations. A unified kingdom arose circa 3200 B.C., and a series of dynasties ruled in Egypt for the next three millennia. The last native dynasty fell to the Persians in 341 B.C., who in turn were replaced by the Greeks, Romans, and Byzantines. It was the Arabs who introduced Islam and the Arabic language in the 7th century and who ruled for the next six centuries. A local military caste, the Mamluks took control about 1250 and continued to govern after the conquest of Egypt by the Ottoman Turks in 1517. Following the completion of the Suez Canal in 1869, Egypt became an important world transportation hub, but also fell heavily into debt. Ostensibly to protect its investments, Britain seized control of Egypt's government in 1882, but nominal allegiance to the Ottoman Empire continued until 1914. Partially independent from the UK in 1922, Egypt acquired full sovereignty with the overthrow of the British-backed monarchy in 1952. The completion of the Aswan High Dam in 1971 and the resultant Lake Nasser have altered the time-honored place of the Nile River in the agriculture and ecology of Egypt. A rapidly growing population (the largest in the Arab world), limited arable land, and dependence on the Nile all continue to overtax resources and stress society. The government has struggled to meet the demands of Egypt's growing population through economic reform and massive investment in communications and physical infrastructure. Egyptian youth and opposition groups, inspired by events in Tunisia leading to overthrow of the government there, organized non-violent demonstrations, marches, and labor strikes in Cairo and other cities throughout Egypt early in 2011. Protester grievances focused on police brutality, state emergency laws, lack of free speech and elections, high unemployment, rising food prices, inflation, and low minimum wages. Pledges by President MUBARAK for the formation of a new government and additional concessions failed to assuage protesters and resulted in an escalation of the number and intensity of demonstrations and clashes with police. In February 2011 MUBARAK resigned and national leadership was assumed by a Supreme Council of Armed Forces (SCAF). The SCAF dissolved the Egyptian parliament, suspended the nation's constitution, and formed a committee to recommend constitutional changes to facilitate a political transition through democratic elections. Following some delays, elections for a new parliament took place between November 2011 and January 2012; however, the lower house of parliament was dissolved in June after a court ruling deemed its formation illegal. Presidential elections held in May and June witnessed the victory of Muslim Brotherhood candidate Mohammed MURSI, but elections to form a new lower house of parliament, scheduled spring 2013, have been put on hold by the Administrative Court in order to review legal arguments over the process used to approve the amended election law.

Chapter 2: Geography

Location:

Northern Africa, bordering the Mediterranean Sea, between Libya and the Gaza Strip, and the Red Sea north of Sudan, and includes the Asian Sinai Peninsula

Geographic coordinates:

27 00 N, 30 00 E

Map references:

Africa

Area:

total: 1,001,450 sq km

country comparison to the world: 30

land: 995,450 sq km

water: 6,000 sq km

Area - comparative:

slightly more than three times the size of New Mexico

Land boundaries:

total: 2,665 km

border countries: Gaza Strip 11 km, Israel 266 km, Libya 1,115 km, Sudan 1,273 km

Coastline:

2,450 km

Maritime claims:

territorial sea: 12 nm

contiguous zone: 24 nm

exclusive economic zone: 200 nm

continental shelf: 200 m depth or to the depth of exploitation

Climate:

desert; hot, dry summers with moderate winters

Terrain:

vast desert plateau interrupted by Nile valley and delta

Elevation extremes:

lowest point: Qattara Depression -133 m

highest point: Mount Catherine 2,629 m

Natural resources:

petroleum, natural gas, iron ore, phosphates, manganese, limestone, gypsum, talc, asbestos, lead, rare earth elements, zinc

Land use:

arable land: 2.87%

permanent crops: 0.79%

other: 96.34% (2011)

Irrigated land:

34,220 sq km (2003)

Total renewable water resources:

57.3 cu km (2011)

Freshwater withdrawal (domestic/industrial/agricultural):

total: 68.3 cu km/yr (8%/6%/86%)

per capita: 973.3 cu m/yr (2000)

Natural hazards:

periodic droughts; frequent earthquakes; flash floods; landslides; hot, driving windstorms called khamsin occur in spring; dust storms; sandstorms

Environment - current issues:

agricultural land being lost to urbanization and windblown sands; increasing soil salination below Aswan High Dam; desertification; oil pollution threatening coral reefs, beaches, and marine habitats; other water pollution from agricultural pesticides, raw sewage, and industrial effluents; limited natural freshwater resources away from the Nile, which is the only perennial water source; rapid growth in population overstraining the Nile and natural resources

Environment - international agreements:

party to: Biodiversity, Climate Change, Climate Change-Kyoto Protocol, Desertification, Endangered Species, Environmental Modification, Hazardous Wastes, Law of the Sea, Marine Dumping, Ozone Layer Protection, Ship Pollution, Tropical Timber 83, Tropical Timber 94, Wetlands

signed, but not ratified: none of the selected agreements

Geography - note:

controls Sinai Peninsula, only land bridge between Africa and remainder of Eastern Hemisphere; controls Suez Canal, a sea link between Indian Ocean and Mediterranean Sea; size, and juxtaposition to Israel, establish its major role in Middle Eastern geopolitics; dependence on upstream neighbors; dominance of Nile basin issues; prone to influxes of refugees from Sudan and the Palestinian territories

Chapter 3: People and Society

Nationality:

noun: Egyptian(s)

adjective: Egyptian

Ethnic groups:

Egyptian 99.6%, other 0.4% (2006 census)

Languages:

Arabic (official), English and French widely understood
by educated classes

Religions:

Muslim (mostly Sunni) 90%, Coptic 9%, other Christian
1%

Population:

85,294,388 (July 2013 est.)

country comparison to the world: 15

Age structure:

0-14 years: 32.3% (male 14,100,807/female 13,474,763)

15-24 years: 18% (male 7,861,197/female 7,471,045)

25-54 years: 38.3% (male 16,565,411/female 16,072,992)

55-64 years: 6.6% (male 2,801,205/female 2,842,786)

65 years and over: 4.8% (male 1,844,456/female
2,259,726) (2013 est.)

Median age:

total: 24.6 years

male: 24.3 years

<u>female</u>: 24.9 years (2012 est.)

Population growth rate:

1.922% (2012 est.)

<u>country comparison to the world</u>: 61

Birth rate:

24.22 births/1,000 population (2012 est.)

<u>country comparison to the world</u>: 67

Death rate:

4.8 deaths/1,000 population (July 2012 est.)

<u>country comparison to the world</u>: 192

Net migration rate:

-0.2 migrant(s)/1,000 population (2012 est.)

<u>country comparison to the world</u>: 123

Urbanization:

<u>urban population</u>: 43.4% of total population (2010)

<u>rate of urbanization</u>: 2.1% annual rate of change (2010-15 est.)

Major cities - population:

CAIRO (capital) 10.902 million; Alexandria 4.387 million (2009)

Sex ratio:

<u>at birth</u>: 1.05 male(s)/female

<u>under 15 years</u>: 1.05 male(s)/female

<u>15-64 years</u>: 1.03 male(s)/female

<u>65 years and over</u>: 0.82 male(s)/female

<u>total population</u>: 1.03 male(s)/female (2011 est.)

Maternal mortality rate:

66 deaths/100,000 live births (2010)

country comparison to the world: 92

Infant mortality rate:

total: 24.23 deaths/1,000 live births

country comparison to the world: 80

male: 25.8 deaths/1,000 live births

female: 22.59 deaths/1,000 live births (2012 est.)

Life expectancy at birth:

total population: 72.93 years

country comparison to the world: 122

male: 70.33 years

female: 75.66 years (2012 est.)

Total fertility rate:

2.9 children born/woman (2013 est.)

country comparison to the world: 65

Health expenditures:

4.7% of GDP (2010)

country comparison to the world: 150

Physicians density:

2.83 physicians/1,000 population (2009)

Hospital bed density:

1.7 beds/1,000 population (2010)

Drinking water source:

improved:

urban: 100% of population

rural: 99% of population

total: 99% of population

unimproved:

urban: 0% of population

rural: 1% of population

total: 1% of population (2010 est.)

Sanitation facility access:

improved:

urban: 97% of population

rural: 93% of population

total: 95% of population

unimproved:

urban: 3% of population

rural: 7% of population

total: 5% of population (2010 est.)

HIV/AIDS - adult prevalence rate:

less than 0.1% (2009 est.)

country comparison to the world: 122

HIV/AIDS - people living with HIV/AIDS:

11,000 (2009 est.)

country comparison to the world: 94

HIV/AIDS - deaths:

fewer than 500 (2009 est.)

country comparison to the world: 84

Major infectious diseases:

degree of risk: intermediate

food or waterborne diseases: bacterial diarrhea, hepatitis A, and typhoid fever

vectorborne disease: Rift Valley fever

water contact disease: schistosomiasis

note: highly pathogenic H5N1 avian influenza has been identified in this country; it poses a negligible risk with extremely rare cases possible among US citizens who have close contact with birds (2009)

Obesity - adult prevalence rate:

30.3% (2006)

country comparison to the world: 8

Children under the age of 5 years underweight:

6.8% (2008)

country comparison to the world: 77

Education expenditures:

3.8% of GDP (2008)

country comparison to the world: 117

Literacy:

definition: age 10 and over can read and write

total population: 72%

male: 80.3%

female: 63.5% (2010 est.)

School life expectancy (primary to tertiary education):

total: 11 years

male: 11 years

female: 11 years (2004)

Unemployment, youth ages 15-24:

total: 24.8%

country comparison to the world: 34

male: 17.2%

female: 47.9% (2007)

Chapter 4: Government and Key Leaders

Country name:

conventional long form: Arab Republic of Egypt

conventional short form: Egypt

local long form: Jumhuriyat Misr al-Arabiyah

local short form: Misr

former: United Arab Republic (with Syria)

Government type:

republic

Capital:

name: Cairo

geographic coordinates: 30 03 N, 31 15 E

time difference: UTC+2 (7 hours ahead of Washington,
DC during Standard Time)

Administrative divisions:

27 governorates (muhafazat, singular - muhafazat); Ad
Daqahliyah, Al Bahr al Ahmar (Red Sea), Al Buhayrah, Al
Fayyum, Al Gharbiyah, Al Iskandariyah (Alexandria), Al
Isma'iliyah (Ismailia), Al Jizah (Giza), Al Minufiyah, Al
Minya, Al Qahirah (Cairo), Al Qalyubiyah, Al Uqsur
(Luxor), Al Wadi al Jadid (New Valley), As Suways
(Suez), Ash Sharqiyah, Aswan, Asyut, Bani Suwayf, Bur
Sa'id (Port Said), Dumyat (Damietta), Janub Sina' (South
Sinai), Kafr ash Shaykh, Matruh, Qina, Shamal Sina'
(North Sinai), Suhaj

Independence:

28 February 1922 (from UK protectorate status; the revolution that began on 23 July 1952 led to a republic being declared on 18 June 1953 and all British troops withdrawn on 18 June 1956); note - it was ca. 3200 B.C. that the Two Lands of Upper (southern) and Lower (northern) Egypt were first united politically

National holiday:

Revolution Day, 23 July (1952)

Constitution:

new constitution passed by referendum 15-22 December 2012, signed by the president 26 December 2012

Legal system:

mixed legal system based on Napoleonic civil law and Islamic religious law; judicial review by Supreme Court and Council of State (oversees validity of administrative decisions)

International law organization participation:

accepts compulsory ICJ jurisdiction with reservations; non-party state to the ICCt

Suffrage:

18 years of age; universal and compulsory

Executive branch:

chief of state: President Muhammad MURSI (since 30 June 2012); vice president (vacant) head of government: Prime Minister Hisham QANDIL (since 24 July 2012)

cabinet: in an early January 2013 cabinet reshuffle, 10 new ministers were sworn in

elections: presidential election (first round held on 23-24 May 2012; runoff held on 16-17 June 2012 (next election NA)

election results: percent of vote (first round) - Mohammed MURSI 24.3%, Ahmed SHAFIQ 23.3%, Hamdin SABAHI 20.4%, Abdul Moneim Aboul FOTOUH 17.2%, Amr MOUSSA 11.1%, other 3.7%; (runoff) - Mohammed MURSI 51.7%, Ahmed SHAFIQ 48.3%

Legislative branch:

bicameral parliament consists of the Shura Council or Majlis al-Shura that traditionally functions mostly in a consultative role (at least 150 seats with up to one-tenth of body appointed by the president to serve six-year terms); and the House of Representatives(at least 350 seats; members elected by popular vote to serve five-year terms)

elections: People's Assembly and Advisory Council elections last held between November and January 2012; elections for new House of Representatives announced for April or May 2013, but probably will be delayed pending decision by the Administrative Court; election for the Shura Council to be held within one year note: the Supreme Court on 14 June 2012 dissolved the People's Assembly

election results: Advisory Council - percent of vote by party - Democratic Alliance for Egypt 45%, Alliance for Egypt (Islamic Bloc) 28.6%, New Wafd Party 8.5%, Egyptian Bloc 5.4%, other 2.8%; seats by party - Democratic Alliance for Egypt 105, Alliance for Egypt (Islamic Bloc) 45, New Wafd Party 14, Egyptian Bloc 8, other 4, independents 4, presidential appointees 90; People's Assembly - percent of vote by party - Democratic Alliance for Egypt 37.5%, Alliance for Egypt (Islamic Bloc) 27.8%, New Wafd Party 9.2%, Egyptian Bloc 8.9%, Al Wasat Party 3.7%, The Revolution Continues Alliance 2.8%, Reform and Development Party 2.2%, National Party of Egypt 1.6%, Freedom Party 1.9%, Egyptian Citizen Party 0.9%, other 3.7; seats by party - Democratic Alliance of Egypt 235, Alliance for Egypt (Islamic Bloc) 123, New Wafd Party 38, Egyptian Bloc 35, Al-Wasat 10, Reform and Development Party 9, The Revolution Continues Alliance 8, National Party of Egypt 5, Egyptian Citizen Party 4, Freedom Party 4, independents 21, other 6, SCAF appointees 10

Judicial branch:

Court of Cassation (final court of appeal in civil and criminal cases); State Council (head of court system

administration); Supreme Constitutional Court
(jurisdiction limited to constitutionality of laws)

Political parties and leaders:

Democratic Alliance for Egypt; Al-Wasat Party;
Constitution Party [Mohammed ELBARADEI];
Democratic Peace Party; Egyptian Citizen Party; Freedom
Party; Nation Party [Hazem Abu ISMAIL]; National Party
of Egypt; New Wafd Party; People's Party; Popular
Current Party [Hamdin SABAHI]; Reform and
Development Party; Revolution Continues Party; Strong
Egypt Party [Abdel Aboul FOTOUH]; The Revolution
Continues Alliance

Political pressure groups and leaders:

NA

International organization participation:

ABEDA, AfDB, AFESD, AMF, AU, BSEC (observer),
CAEU, CD, CICA, COMESA, D-8, EBRD, FAO, G-15,
G-24, G-77, IAEA, IBRD, ICAO, ICC (national
committees), ICRM, IDA, IDB, IFAD, IFC, IFRCS, IHO,
ILO, IMF, IMO, IMSO, Interpol, IOC, IOM, IPU, ISO,
ITSO, ITU, LAS, MIGA, MINURSO, MONUSCO, NAM,
OAPEC, OAS (observer), OIC, OIF, OSCE (partner),
PCA, UN, UNAMID, UNCTAD, UNESCO, UNHCR,
UNIDO, UNISFA, UNMIL, UNMISS, UNOCI, UNRWA,
UNWTO, UPU, WCO, WFTU (NGOs), WHO, WIPO,
WMO, WTO

Diplomatic representation in the US:

chief of mission: Ambassador Mohamed TAWFIK

chancery: 3521 International Court NW, Washington, DC
20008

telephone: [1] (202) 895-5400

FAX: [1] (202) 244-5131

consulate(s) general: Chicago, Houston, Los Angeles, New
York

Diplomatic representation from the US:

chief of mission: Ambassador Ann W. PATTERSON

embassy: 5 Tawfik Diab St., Garden City, Cairo

mailing address: Unit 64900, Box 15, APO AE 09839-
4900; 5 Tawfik Diab Street, Garden City, Cairo

telephone: [20] (2) 2797-3300

FAX: [20] (2) 2797-3200

Key Leaders:

Pres.	Muhammad MURSI
Vice Pres.	
Prime Min.	Hisham QANDIL
Min. of Agriculture & Land Reclamation	Mohamed Salah Abdel MO'MEN
Min. of Antiquities	Mohamed Ibrahim ALI
Min. of Awqaf (Religious Affairs)	Talaat AFIFI
Min. of Civil Aviation	Wael MADAWY

Min. of Communications & Information Technology	Atef HELMY
Min. of Culture	
Min. of Defense	Abdelfattah Said ELSISI, *Lt. Gen.*
Min. of Education	Ibrahim Ahmed Ghoneim DEIF
Min. of Electricity & Energy	Ahmed IMAM
Min. of Finance	El-Mursi HEGAZY
Min. of Foreign Affairs	Mohamed Kamel AMR
Min. of Foreign Trade & Industry	Hatem SALEH
Min. of Health & Population	Mohamed Hamed MUSTAFA
Min. of Higher Education	Moustafa MOSAD
Min. of Housing, Utilities, & Urban Communities	Tarek WAFIQ
Min. of Information	Salah Abdel MAQSOOD
Min. of Interior	Mohamed IBRAHIM
Min. of Intl. Cooperation & Planning	Ashraf AL ARABY
Min. of Irrigation & Water Resources	Mohamed Baha AL DIN AHMED
Min. of Justice	Ahmed MEKKY
Min. of Legal Affairs & Parliamentary Councils	Omar SALEM

Min. of Manpower & Immigration	Khaled Mahmoud AL AZHARY
Min. of Military Production	Abdelfattah Said ELSISI, *Lt. Gen.*
Min. of Petroleum & Metallurgical Wealth	Osama KAMAL
Min. of Science, Technology, & Scientific Research	Nadia ZAKHARY
Min. of Social Affairs & Insurance	Nagwa KHALIL
Min. of Sport	El Amry FAROUK
Min. of Supply & Internal Trade	Bassem Kamel OUDA
Min. of Tourism	Hisham ZAAZOU
Min. of Transport	Hatem Abdel LATIF
Min. of Youth	Osama YASSIN
Min. of State for Environmental Affairs	Khaled FAHMY
Min. of State for Local Development	Mohamed Ali BISHR
Min. of State for Military Production	Reda Hafiz AL-MAJID, *Air Mar.*
Governor, Central Bank of Egypt	Hisham RAMEZ

Ambassador to the US	Mohamed TAWFIK
Permanent Representative to the UN, New York	Mootaz Ahmadein KHALIL

Flag description:

three equal horizontal bands of red (top), white, and black; the national emblem (a gold Eagle of Saladin facing the hoist side with a shield superimposed on its chest above a scroll bearing the name of the country in Arabic) centered in the white band; the band colors derive from the Arab Liberation flag and represent oppression (black), overcome through bloody struggle (red), to be replaced by a bright future (white)

note: similar to the flag of Syria, which has two green stars in the white band, Iraq, which has an Arabic inscription centered in the white band, and Yemen, which has a plain white band

National symbol(s):

golden eagle

National anthem:

name: "Bilady, Bilady, Bilady" (My Homeland, My Homeland, My Homeland)

lyrics/music: Younis-al QADI/Sayed DARWISH

note: adopted 1979; after the signing of the 1979 peace with Israel, Egypt sought to create an anthem less militaristic than its previous one; Sayed DARWISH, commonly considered the father of modern Egyptian music, composed the anthem

Chapter 5: Economy

Economy - overview:

Occupying the northeast corner of the African continent,
Egypt is bisected by the highly fertile Nile valley, where
most economic activity takes place. Egypt's economy was
highly centralized during the rule of former President
Gamal Abdel NASSER but opened up considerably under
former Presidents Anwar EL-SADAT and Mohamed
Hosni MUBARAK. Cairo from 2004 to 2008 aggressively
pursued economic reforms to attract foreign investment
and facilitate GDP growth. Despite the relatively high
levels of economic growth in recent years, living
conditions for the average Egyptian remained poor and
contributed to public discontent. After unrest erupted in
January 2011, the Egyptian Government backtracked on
economic reforms, drastically increasing social spending
to address public dissatisfaction, but political uncertainty
at the same time caused economic growth to slow
significantly, reducing the government's revenues.
Tourism, manufacturing, and construction were among the
hardest hit sectors of the Egyptian economy, and economic
growth is likely to remain slow during the next several
years. The government drew down foreign exchange
reserves by more than 50% in 2011 and 2012 to support
the Egyptian pound and the dearth of foreign financial

assistance - as a result of unsuccessful negotiations with the International Monetary Fund over a multi-billion dollar loan agreement which have dragged on more than 20 months - could precipitate fiscal and balance of payments crises in 2013.

GDP (purchasing power parity):

$537.8 billion (2012 est.)

country comparison to the world: 27

$527.4 billion (2011 est.)

$518.2 billion (2010 est.)

note: data are in 2012 US dollars

GDP (official exchange rate):

$255 billion (2012 est.)

GDP - real growth rate:

2% (2012 est.)

country comparison to the world: 138

1.8% (2011 est.)

5.1% (2010 est.)

GDP - per capita (PPP):

$6,600 (2012 est.)

country comparison to the world: 140

$6,600 (2011 est.)

$6,600 (2010 est.)

note: data are in 2012 US dollars

GDP - composition by sector:

agriculture: 14.7%

industry: 37.4%

services: 47.9% (2012 est.)

Labor force:

27.24 million (2012 est.)

country comparison to the world: 22

Labor force - by occupation:

agriculture: 32%

industry: 17%

services: 51% (2001 est.)

Unemployment rate:

12.5% (2012 est.)

country comparison to the world: 130

12% (2011 est.)

Population below poverty line:

20% (2005 est.)

Household income or consumption by percentage share:

lowest 10%: 3.9%

highest 10%: 27.6% (2005)

Distribution of family income - Gini index:

34.4 (2001)

country comparison to the world: 90

Investment (gross fixed):

13.5% of GDP (2012 est.)

country comparison to the world: 141

Budget:

revenues: $56.64 billion

expenditures: $83.24 billion (2012 est.)

Taxes and other revenues:

22.2% of GDP (2012 est.)

country comparison to the world: 140

Budget surplus (+) or deficit (-):

-10.4% of GDP (2012 est.)

country comparison to the world: 206

Public debt:

85% of GDP (2012 est.)

country comparison to the world: 21

83.6% of GDP (2011 est.)

note: data cover central government debt, and includes debt instruments issued (or owned) by government entities other than the treasury; the data include treasury debt held by foreign entities; the data include debt issued by subnational entities, as well as intra-governmental debt; intra-governmental debt consists of treasury borrowings from surpluses in the social funds, such as for retirement, medical care, and unemployment; debt instruments for the social funds are sold at public auctions

Inflation rate (consumer prices):

8.5% (2012 est.)

country comparison to the world: 189

10.2% (2011 est.)

Central bank discount rate:

8.68% (31 December 2010 est.)

country comparison to the world: 31
8.5% (31 December 2009 est.)

Commercial bank prime lending rate:

12.5% (31 December 2012 est.)

country comparison to the world: 76

11.03% (31 December 2011 est.)

Stock of narrow money:

$47.73 billion (31 December 2012 est.)

country comparison to the world: 48

$42.25 billion (31 December 2011 est.)

Stock of broad money:

$192.5 billion (31 December 2012 est.)

country comparison to the world: 42

$171.7 billion (31 December 2011 est.)

Stock of domestic credit:

$178.4 billion (31 December 2012 est.)

country comparison to the world: 42

$169.1 billion (31 December 2011 est.)

Market value of publicly traded shares:

$48.68 billion (31 December 2011)

country comparison to the world: 45

$82.49 billion (31 December 2010)

$89.95 billion (31 December 2009)

Agriculture - products:

cotton, rice, corn, wheat, beans, fruits, vegetables; cattle, water buffalo, sheep, goats

Industries:

textiles, food processing, tourism, chemicals, pharmaceuticals, hydrocarbons, construction, cement, metals, light manufactures

Industrial production growth rate:

0.5% (2011 est.)

country comparison to the world: 138

Current account balance:

-$8.417 billion (2012 est.)

country comparison to the world: 173

-$6.521 billion (2011 est.)

Exports:

$28.37 billion (2012 est.)

country comparison to the world: 67

$27.91 billion (2011 est.)

Exports - commodities:

crude oil and petroleum products, cotton, textiles, metal products, chemicals, processed food

Exports - partners:

Italy 8.7%, India 7.3%, Saudi Arabia 6.1%, US 5.2%, Turkey 4.9%, Spain 4.2%, France 4.2% (2011)

Imports:

$58.76 billion (2012 est.)

country comparison to the world: 50

$55.07 billion (2011 est.)

Imports - commodities:

machinery and equipment, foodstuffs, chemicals, wood products, fuels

Imports - partners:

US 10.7%, China 9.1%, Germany 6.3%, Italy 5.1%, Kuwait 4.7%, Turkey 4.4%, Saudi Arabia 4.3% (2011)

Reserves of foreign exchange and gold:

$15.26 billion (31 December 2012 est.)

country comparison to the world: 66

$17.66 billion (31 December 2011 est.)

Debt - external:

$34.88 billion (31 December 2012 est.)

country comparison to the world: 66

$33.75 billion (31 December 2011 est.)

Stock of direct foreign investment - at home:

$73.81 billion (31 December 2012 est.)

country comparison to the world: 48

$72.61 billion (31 December 2011 est.)

Stock of direct foreign investment - abroad:

$6.824 billion (31 December 2012 est.)

country comparison to the world: 59

$6.074 billion (31 December 2011 est.)

Exchange rates:

Egyptian pounds (EGP) per US dollar -

6.05 (2012 est.)

5.9358 (2011 est.)

5.6219 (2010 est.)

5.545 (2009)

5.4 (2008)

Fiscal year:

1 July - 30 June

Chapter 6: Energy

Electricity - production:

136 6 billion kWh (2010 est.)

country comparison to the world: 28

Electricity - consumption:

115 8 billion kWh (2009 est.)

country comparison to the world: 28

Electricity - exports:

1.118 billion kWh (2009 est.)

country comparison to the world: 54

Electricity - imports:

183 million kWh (2009 est.)

country comparison to the world: 89

Electricity - installed generating capacity:

24.67 million kW (2009 est.)

country comparison to the world: 34

Electricity - from fossil fuels:

86.9% of total installed capacity (2009 est.)

country comparison to the world: 84

Electricity - from nuclear fuels:

0% of total installed capacity (2009 est.)

country comparison to the world: 81

Electricity - from hydroelectric plants:

11.4% of total installed capacity (2009 est.)

country comparison to the world: 113

Electricity - from other renewable sources:

1.7% of total installed capacity (2009 est.)

country comparison to the world: 65

Crude oil - production:

711,500 bbl/day (2011 est.)

country comparison to the world: 28

Crude oil - exports:

86,720 bbl/day (2009 est.)

country comparison to the world: 40

Crude oil - imports:

48,590 bbl/day (2009 est.)

country comparison to the world: 57

Crude oil - proved reserves:

4.45 billion bbl (1 January 2013 est.)

country comparison to the world: 28

Refined petroleum products - production:

628,100 bbl/day (2008 est.)

country comparison to the world: 30

Refined petroleum products - consumption:

816,300 bbl/day (2011 est.)

country comparison to the world: 24

Refined petroleum products - exports:

91,680 bbl/day (2008 est.)

country comparison to the world: 44

Refined petroleum products - imports:

114,600 bbl/day (2008 est.)

country comparison to the world: 45

Natural gas - production:

61.33 billion cu m (2010 est.)

country comparison to the world: 16

Natural gas - consumption:

46.16 billion cu m (2010 est.)

country comparison to the world: 19

Natural gas - exports:

15.17 billion cu m (2010 est.)

country comparison to the world: 19

Natural gas - imports:

0 cu m (2010 est.)

country comparison to the world: 187

Natural gas - proved reserves:

2.186 trillion cu m (1 January 2012 est.)

country comparison to the world: 17

Carbon dioxide emissions from consumption of energy:

196.5 million Mt (2010 est.)

country comparison to the world: 28

Chapter 7: Communications

Telephones - main lines in use:

8.714 million (2011)

country comparison to the world: 23

Telephones - mobile cellular:

83.425 million (2011)

country comparison to the world: 16

Telephone system:

general assessment: underwent extensive upgrading during 1990s; principal centers at Alexandria, Cairo, Al Mansurah, Ismailia, Suez, and Tanta are connected by coaxial cable and microwave radio relay

domestic: largest fixed-line system in the region; as of 2011 there were multiple mobile-cellular networks with a total of roughly 83 million subscribers

international: country code - 20; landing point for Aletar, the SEA-ME-WE-3 and SEA-ME-WE-4 submarine cable networks, Link Around the Globe (FLAG) Falcon and FLAG FEA; satellite earth stations - 4 (2 Intelsat - Atlantic Ocean and Indian Ocean, 1 Arabsat, and 1 Inmarsat); tropospheric scatter to Sudan; microwave radio relay to Israel; a participant in Medarabtel (2011)

Broadcast media:

mix of state-run and private broadcast media; state-run TV operates 2 national and 6 regional terrestrial networks as we.l as a few satellite channels; about 20 private satellite channels and a large number of Arabic satellite channels are available via subscription; state-run radio operates about 70 stations belonging to 8 networks; 2 privately-owned radio stations operational (2008)

Internet country code:

.eg

Internet hosts:

200,430 (2012)

country comparison to the world: 71

Internet users:

20.136 million (2009)

country comparison to the world: 21

Chapter 8: Transportation

Airports:

84 (2012)

country comparison to the world: 66

Airports - with paved runways:

total: 72

over 3,047 m: 15

2,438 to 3,047 m: 36

1,524 to 2,437 m: 15

under 914 m: 6 (2012)

Airports - with unpaved runways:

total: 12

2,438 to 3,047 m: 1

1,524 to 2,437 m: 3

914 to 1,523 m: 5

under 914 m: 3 (2012)

Heliports:

6 (2012)

Pipelines:

condensate 320 km; condensate/gas 13 km; gas 6,628 km; liquid petroleum gas 956 km; oil 4,332 km; oil/gas/water 3 km; refined products 895 km; water 13 km (2010)

Railways:

total: 5,083 km

country comparison to the world: 34

standard gauge: 5,083 km 1.435-m gauge (62 km electrified) (2009)

Roadways:

total: 65,050 km

country comparison to the world: 69

paved: 47,500 km

unpaved: 17.550 km (2009)

Waterways:

3,500 km (includes the Nile River, Lake Nasser, Alexandria-Cairo Waterway, and numerous smaller canals in Nile Delta; the Suez Canal (193.5 km including approaches) is navigable by oceangoing vessels drawing up to 17.68 m) (2011)

country comparison to the world: 30

Merchant marine:

total: 67

country comparison to the world: 62

by type: bulk carrier 16, cargo 20, container 3, passenger/cargo 7, petroleum tanker 12, roll on/roll off 9

foreign-owned: 13 (Denmark 1, France 1, Greece 8, Jordan 2, Lebanon 1)

registered in other countries: 42 (Cambodia 4, Georgia 7, Honduras 2. Liberia 3, Malta 1, Marshall Islands 1, Moldova 5. Panama 11, Saint Kitts and Nevis 1, Saint Vincent and the Grenadines 2, Saudi Arabia 1, Sierra Leone 3, unknown 1) (2010)

Ports and terminals:

Ayn Sukhnah, Alexandria, Damietta, El Dekheila, Port Said, Sidi Kurayr, Suez

Chapter 9: Military

Military branches:

Army, Navy, Egyptian Air Force (Al-Quwwat al-Jawwiya il-Misriya), Egyptian Air Defense Command (2013)

Military service age and obligation:

18-30 years of age for male conscript military service; service obligation - 18-36 months, followed by a 9-year reserve obligation; voluntary enlistment possible from age 16 (2012)

Manpower available for military service:

males age 16-49: 21,012,199

females age 16-49: 20,145,021 (2010 est.)

Manpower fit for military service:

males age 16-49: 18,060,543

females age 16-49: 17,244,838 (2010 est.)

Manpower reaching militarily significant age annually:

male: 783,405

female: 748,647 (2010 est.)

Military expenditures:

2.2% of GDP (2012)

country comparison to the world: 62

Chapter 10: Transnational Issues

Disputes - international:

Sudan claims but Egypt de facto administers security and economic development of Halaib region north of the 22nd parallel boundary; Egypt no longer shows its administration of the Bir Tawil trapezoid in Sudan on its maps; Gazan breaches in the security wall with Egypt in January 2008 highlight difficulties in monitoring the Sinai border; Saudi Arabia claims Egyptian-administered islands of Tiran and Sanafir

Refugees and internally displaced persons:

refugees (country of origin): 70,029 (West Bank and Gaza Strip); 10,324 (Sudan); 6,037 (Iraq) (2011); 48,782 (Syria); 7,595 (Somalia) (2013)

Illicit drugs:

transit point for cannabis, heroin, and opium moving to Europe, Israel, and North Africa; transit stop for Nigerian drug couriers; concern as money laundering site due to lax enforcement of financial regulations

Map of Egypt

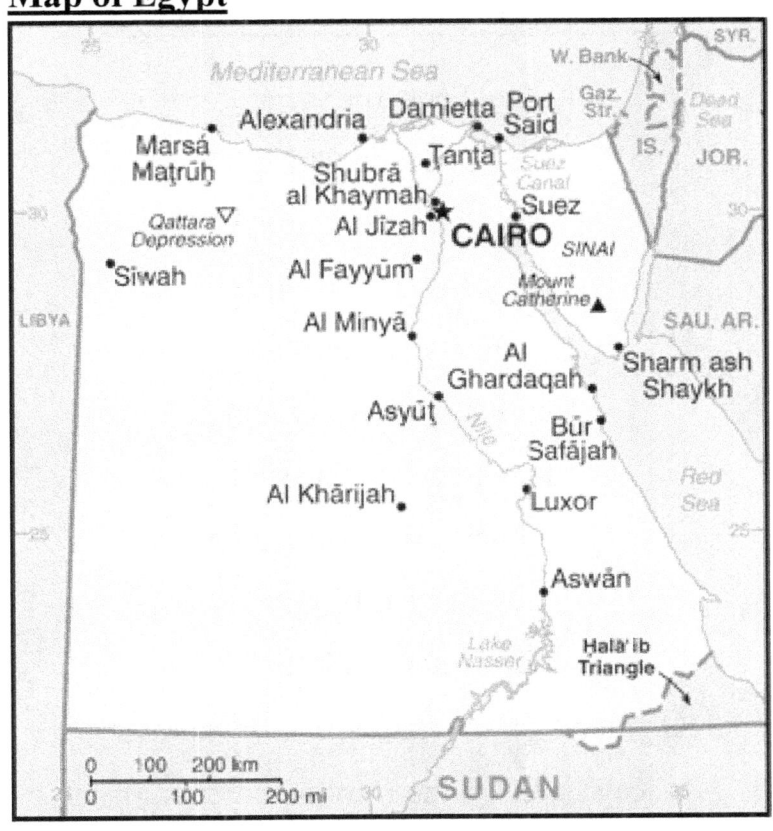

Other Key Facts™ Titles

Key Facts on South Korea

Key Facts on France

Key Facts on the United Kingdom

All Key Facts™ Titles are Available at

www.Amazon.com

THE INTERNATIONALIST®

2013

WWW.INTERNATIONALIST.COM

www.ingramcontent.com/pod-product-compliance
Lightning Source LLC
Chambersburg PA
CBHW071649170526
45166CB00003B/1496